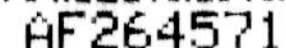

AF264571

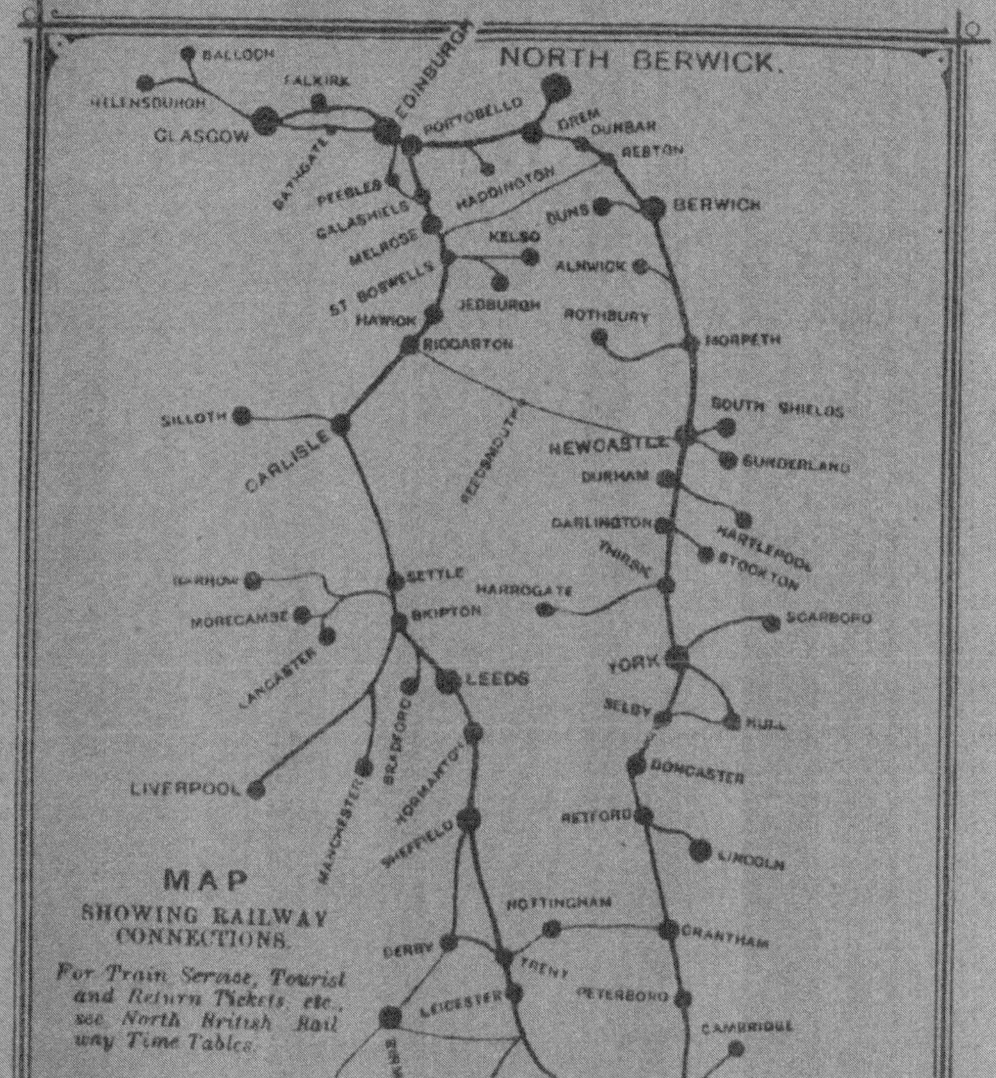

NORTH BERWICK.
BALLOCH
FALKIRK
HELENSBURGH
GLASGOW
BATHGATE
EDINBURGH
PORTOBELLO
DREM
DUNBAR
RESTON
PEEBLES
HADDINGTON
GALASHIELS
DUNS
BERWICK
MELROSE
KELSO
ST BOSWELLS
ALNWICK
JEDBURGH
ROTHBURY
HAWICK
RIOCARTON
MORPETH
SILLOTH
SOUTH SHIELDS
NEWCASTLE
CARLISLE
BEDSMOUTH
SUNDERLAND
DURHAM
DARLINGTON
HARTLEPOOL
THIRSK
STOCKTON
BARROW
SETTLE
HARROGATE
MORECAMBE
SKIPTON
SCARBORO
LANCASTER
LEEDS
YORK
BRADFORD
SELBY
HULL
LIVERPOOL
NORMANTON
DONCASTER
MANCHESTER
RETFORD
SHEFFIELD
LINCOLN
MAP
SHOWING RAILWAY
CONNECTIONS.
NOTTINGHAM
For Train Service, Tourist
and Return Tickets, etc.,
see North British Rail
way Time Tables.
DERBY
GRANTHAM
TRENT
LEICESTER
PETERBORO
CAMBRIDGE
BIRMINGHAM
RUGBY
BEDFORD
HITCHEN
BRISTOL
ST PANCRAS
KING'S CROSS
BATH
LONDON

MARINE HOTEL

GUIDE

TO

NORTH BERWICK

AND VICINITY.

FIFTH EDITION.

ENTERED AT STATIONERS' HALL.

Printed by

GEO. STEWART & CO.,

92 GEORGE STREET, EDINBURGH,

AND AT LONDON.

1891.

PREFACE.

THIS little Handbook is issued as a concise and useful description of a unique and charming Watering-place. Any stranger who may be tempted thither by the description of its varied attractions will, we are sure, feel grateful for thus being introduced to it. Those who already know it well, will here find much useful information in a handy form.

CONTENTS.

MARINE HOTEL, NORTH BERWICK.

W. NIEBECKER, Manager,
Late Manager of the Alexandra and St James' Hotels, London.

NORTH BERWICK.

S Edinburgh occupies the proud position of the "Modern Athens," so Scotland's principal watering-place, North Berwick, is justly called the "Biarritz of the North"; indeed, but few watering-places in Scotland, and certainly none on the east coast, can for a moment compare with it in its many attractions. To the lover of nature it possesses charms of beauty of scenery ever changing and ever new; to the dwellers in cities, jaded with the hurry and bustle of business life, and to the younger generation, so glad to escape from the monotony of school, its fresh, invigorating air—always cool and bracing, when the streets of the towns, and even the country inland, are baking with the summer heat—brings new life and strength. In the beautiful and varied colouring of the rocks, islands, and shore, in the lovely effects of the sea, sky, and brilliant sunset, or among the many picturesque and shady nooks in the woods around, the artist is never at a loss in finding some charming subject for his pencil. But not less than its natural attractions are the varied amusements visitors can find to wile away the time. With Scotsmen, the first place, of course, must be given to the National Game, and certainly no golfing links in the kingdoms surpass those of North Berwick, either in the facilities they afford for good play, in the fine order in which they are at all times kept, or in the skill shown by the many players who frequent them. Judging from our own experience, the game seems all-satisfying to the golfers; but as other visitors will require other attractions, they can find plenty in the numerous interesting and picturesque walks and drives; in the fine sea-bathing; in boating excursions to the Bass Rock, or the other islands which lie off the coast; or, if simply inclined for rest and quiet, they can wander along the sea-shore, or rest on the beach, lulled by the plash of the waves, or watch the passing of the many vessels sailing and arriving from all parts of the globe. The little folks, in their turn, cannot wish for anything better than to scamper over the breezy links, gathering daisies and buttercups, oxlips and cowslips, or, with spade and bucket, to build castles of the hard, firm sand, or to explore the little pools among the rocks, left by the receding tide, which teem with curiosities of marine life— which latter pursuit will be found full of interest to children of a larger growth as well. Here are delicately-tinted sea-weeds in numberless variety, shells with their living inhabitants, the quarrelsome crabs (which require agile fingers to pull them out without getting a sharp nip or two), the curious little hermit-crabs, brilliant anemones, the beautiful little *cyprœa*, or cowrie, and numbers of little fish, that dart in and out among the stones to avoid capture. The variety of shells that can be collected on the shore is also another source of great interest to the children, and here and there a pebble may be found by the diligent seeker. Altogether, visitors to North Berwick, young and old, need never feel time hang heavy on their hands.

Situated about twenty-two miles east of Edinburgh, at the entrance to the Firth of Forth, the town of North Berwick stretches along the sea-shore for about a mile, and extends also up the slopes behind. Between the houses and the sea, for a breadth of about 200 yards, and a length of several miles, are the celebrated Golfing Links—a series of low-lying downs, covered with short, fine grass, and broken with small sandy hillocks and hollows, which form the obstacles the golfer takes such pride in overcoming. Looking seawards we have a beautiful view over the Firth of Forth, and out to the broad expanse of the German Ocean.

On the opposite side is the lone undulating line of the Fifeshire coast, broken to the east by the Isle of May, and to the north and west overshadowed by the distant Ochil and Lomond ranges. Close at hand rise out of the sea the rocky islets of Fidra, The Lamb, and Craigleith, and, towering over all, the stupendous Bass Rock, impressive and fascinating alike in its weird and lonely grandeur, and in its stirring and eventful history. Immediately behind the town, to the south, rises North Berwick Law—the first of that curious series of isolated rocky hills which stretch from the Forth to the Clyde, of which the principle other examples are the rocks of Edinburgh and Stirling Castles and Dumbarton Rock. Inland the environs of North Berwick are prettily diversified with woods, pastures, and well-kept farms, the agricultural district in the neighbourhood being one of the most fertile in the kingdom. The residences of the nobility and gentry in the vicinity are numerous, and many of them exceedingly picturesque and beautifully situated, and most of their owners are exceedingly courteous in permitting strangers to see through the mansions or walk and drive through the parks.

The climate of North Berwick is comparatively mild and equable in the winter, spring, and autumn months. The bitter steely winds that are often so unpleasant in Edinburgh seem tempered here, which may doubtless be greatly owing to the higher elevation occupied by the city. In summer the climate is delightful, there being very rarely, owing to the fresh sea breezes, a day that may be called in the least oppressive, while the ozone from the sea-shore makes the air always invigorating and health-restoring. Under these circumstances the air is necessarily " strong," and often, for the first two days or so, especially among children, a certain sleepiness and sense of fatigue are felt, which, however, soon pass off, and are replaced by an almost inexhaustible fund of energy and cheerfulness, and certainly a wonderful appetite. Indeed, after a week at North Berwick, one can really say, " Life is worth living."

The reliable Statistics prove the healthiness of the place, and the supply of water from the Lammermoor Hills, a distance of 12 miles, is the best in the kingdom, The sanitary arrangements and drainage are modern, and very perfect.

The society at North Berwick is exceedingly good, and pleasant withal, being entirely free from the display of an ultra-fashionable watering-place. The visitors belong almost entirely to the better classes of society, and North Berwick has the great advantage of being quite free from invasions of " cheap-trippers."

ROUTES TO NORTH BERWICK.

Besides being one of the most attractive, North Berwick is one of the most accessible of the important Scottish watering-places. From Edinburgh express trains run through in thirty-five minutes, and from Glasgow in about two hours. From London, and all stations in the east of England, there is direct communication, *via* Drem, by the North British and Great Northern Railways; from the midland counties by the Midland Railway, *via* York, Berwick, and Drem; or from the northern counties, *via* Newcastle, Berwick, and Drem. Travellers from Liverpool, Manchester, and other towns in the west of England, must come through Edinburgh, whence, as we have said, they can reach North Berwick in thirty-five minutes.

GENERAL DESCRIPTION.

The origin of the name North Berwick—so called to distinguish it from Berwick-on-Tweed, or South Berwick, as it was originally called—is very uncertain, being variously supposed to have been derived from *Bare Wick*, a bare or exposed village, supposed to have reference to its open position on the sea coast ; or from a contraction of *Aber Wick*—*aber* signifying the mouth of a stream, and *wick* a village, of which we have other instances, as in Aberdeen at the mouth of the Dee, &c. The latter derivation, however, could only have applied to Berwick-on-Tweed.

The origin of the town—unquestionably of very ancient date—is lost in obscurity. The town was first incorporated by a charter of Robert III. at the close of the fourteenth century, and its privileges were renewed and confirmed by a second charter, granted by James VI. in 1568. During the twelfth and thirteenth centuries the town and manorial rights were in the possession of the Earls of Fife, descendants of Macduff. In the fourteenth century the manor passed to William, Earl of Douglas, but was forfeited in 1455 by his descendant, James Earl of Douglas. In 1479 James III. restored the estate to Archibald, Earl of Angus, known as " Bell the

Cat," heir of Earl James, in the possession of whose descendants it remained till the commencement of last century, when the barony and estate were sold to Sir Hew Dalrymple, Lord President of the Court of Session, to whose lineal descendant, the present Baronet, Sir Walter Hamilton Dalrymple, they still belong.

In the Scottish Parliament North Berwick was represented by its own Commissioner, and since the Union has sent a Member to the Parliament of the United Kingdom, along with the other Haddington Burghs. The population in 1881 was 2688, and at present the annual number of visitors is over 20,000.

For these visitors ample accommodation is provided by the hotels, lodging-houses, and villas. The largest and best hotel is the

MARINE HOTEL,

one of the finest hotels in Scotland, a handsome modern erection, surrounded by its own grounds, and commanding a beautiful view of the whole estuary of the Forth, with the Fife coast and Ochil range in the distance, while in the foreground are the celebrated Links, which intervene between the hotel and the sea, and the rocky and picturesque islands of The Bass, Fidra, Lamb, and Craigleith. The building, which is in handsome Scottish Baronial style, was erected in 1876, at a cost of £35,000. Additions were made in 1881 at a further expense of £10,000, and the hotel is now one of the best equipped and most elegantly furnished establishments in the kingdom, being fitted with every modern convenience for the use and comfort of visitors. The public rooms, which are lofty, spacious, and comfortable, comprise coffee-room, drawing-room (well supplied with books and periodicals), billiard and smoking rooms. The bedrooms are, without exception, large, airy, and well furnished.

The grounds surrounding the hotel are prettily laid out, with excellent lawns for tennis, &c.

The baths are extensively and luxuriously fitted up, and are supplied with salt water drawn direct from the sea. Hot, cold, douche, spray, and medicated baths, both salt and fresh, can be had on the shortest notice.

A modern steam laundry is attached to the hotel.

The *cuisine* is unexceptionable, and the *table d'hôte*, served at separate tables from 6 to 8, is well known for its uniform excellence.

Post and Telegraph Office in the Hotel.

The proprietor spares no expense or trouble in making the hotel one of the most comfortable, as it is undoubtedly one of the most attractive, seaside establishments in the kingdom.

During the winter the building is thoroughly warmed and kept at equal temperature, and every arrangement made to make the hotel a most agreeable and pleasant winter residence. (*See Press Notices, page* 50.)

MARINE HOTEL FROM THE LINKS.

B

In describing shortly the various points of interest in the town, we must first notice the

HIGH STREET,

the principal thoroughfare, which, though narrow, is of considerable length, running east and west. The only house of particular interest in the street is an old mansion on the north side, which is described in James Grant's stirring romance of " The White Cockade " as being the residence of Bailie Reuben M'Craftie. " Still conspicuous by its ancient appearance, it stands opposite a building which was *then* an inn or change-house, and bore the Otterburn arms creaking in the wind from an iron rod."

Crossing the High Street at right angles is *Quality Street*, the broadest and finest street in the town, and doubtless originally so called from the residences of the gentry or " quality" having been situated here. The old houses have, however, been pulled down and replaced by modern buildings, with the exception of a long old-fashioned building on the east side, half hidden by trees, which in the original title-deeds is described as the " Tower of Babel." At the south-east corner of High and Quality Streets is a plain barn-like structure, to which but few would suppose pertained the dignity of being the *Town Hall*. Here is still preserved the old parish stocks in which drunkards and others convicted of petty offences were veritably held in limbo. At the south end of Quality Street is the old residence of the Dalrymple family, which is now occupied by Sir Walter Hamilton Dalrymple, Bart.

THE AULD KIRK.

Prominent among the relics of a bygone age are the ruins of the Auld Kirk, which stand on a slight eminence near the harbour. These ruins of the ancient Parish Church, from the pulpit of which a local tradition tells us that Satan held forth to the witches of the Bass, were formerly on an islet connected with the shore by a Bridge, as an entry in the Kirk Session books tells us—"That it has been resolved rather to change the site of the Church than to rebuild the arches or bridges connecting the Kirk with the shore." The date of the erection of the Church is unknown, but it certainly antedated the Reformation. On this islet was the old Parish Burial-Ground; but the only relic we have of this ancient place of sepulture is a large flat stone, which is supposed to mark the burial place of the Lauders of the Bass. In 1788, in one of the vaults of the Auld Kirk, a seal was found bearing the legend "Sigillium Willilmi de Douglas," which may quite probably have been the seal of the first Lord of the Manor, William, Earl of Douglas.

THE ABBEY.

On the south side of the Railway Station, about a quarter of a mile from the town, are the picturesque ruins of a Cistercian Nunnery, founded by Duncan, fifth Earl of Fife, about the middle of the twelfth century. This Nunnery, which was one of the most important south of the Forth, was dedicated to the Virgin Mary, and richly endowed with revenues from lands in the counties of Berwick, Fife, Edinburgh, Roxburgh, Linlithgow, and Ayr. It besides possessed the patronage of the Parish Church of North Berwick, and the advowson of the Church of Largo. During the English invasion of 1296, the Abbess submitted to, and obtained the protection of, Edward I. During the reign of James III. the wealth of the Abbey, and the defenceless condition of its inmates, led to its being plundered, and the nuns and their domestics being brutally ill-treated. The Abbess, however, on appealing to the Scottish Parliament, obtained full redress, the revenues of the Abbey being restored, and the assailants condemned to make good the damages the Abbey had suffered. During the reign of James IV. a daughter of Sir Patrick Home of Polwarth became Abbess, and she was succeeded by her niece Isabella, daughter of Sir Alexander Home. This connection of the Home family with the Abbey led to its revenues being given to Sir Alexander on the suppression of the Monasteries at the Reformation, at which period the Abbey contained eleven nuns, with an income of £20 per annum each. One of the customs of the nuns was to make an annual pilgrimage to the Island of Fidra, where fragments of their little chapel are still to be seen.

The Abbey was originally of considerable size, and extended over a space of nearly one acre; but the present ruins though exceedingly picturesque, give but little idea

of its former magnificence.   They consist of portions of the refectory, the kitchen (with a fine old fireplace), and at the east end a portion of the chapel.   The fragment of an arch, standing at some distance from the ruins, was part of the original entrance gateway.   Many antiquarian remains of pottery, weapons, urns, and fragments of large leaden pipes, which, doubtless, conveyed water to the Abbey, have been dug up at various times.   The most important discovery was made in 1848 during the construction of the branch of the North British Railway to North Berwick, when two stone coffins were discovered.   These sarcophagi, which were about four feet in length, each contained a human skeleton, beside one of which were an iron sword and dagger.   Many other antiquarian remains have also been discovered in the neighbourhood of North Berwick, among which have been several very curious tobacco pipes of clay, which are supposed to have been used as early as the Celtic period for smoking dried herbs.   Sir Walter Scott, in " Marmion," describes the Abbess of St Hilda as staying at this Abbey, while Marmion and Clara went on to Tantallon Castle.

> " And now, when close at hand they saw
> North Berwick's town, and lofty Law,
> Fitz-Eustace bade them pause a while,
> Before a venerable pile,
>   Whose turrets view'd, afar,
> The lofty Bass, the Lambie Isle,
>   The ocean's peace or war."
>
> *Canto V. xxix.*

CHURCHES.

The PARISH CHURCH OF ST ANDREW is situated in the principal street of the town. The first church of North Berwick was probably founded by St Baldred of the Bass in the seventeenth century. The district was formed into a parish before 1154, and the old Church of St Andrew, near the Harbour, of which a porch remains, may have been built about that time. It continued to be the Parish Church till the middle of the seventeenth century, when it was superseded by the church the ruins of which stand in the Churchyard. This was opened in 1664, and used for the last time in June 1883, when the present church of St Andrew was set apart for public worship. It is built in the early English Gothic style, and the design provides for a tower and steeple. The church accommodates about 800. It contains three fine memorial windows, in memory of members of the Suttie family of Balgone, and a good organ, built by Forster & Andrews, Organ Builders, Hull. The oak pew in the east transept was made from the patron's gallery in the old church, and is said to have been taken previously from Tantallon Castle. Hours of service, 11.15 A.M. and 6 P.M. Parish Minister, Rev. G. W. Sprott, D.D.

The FREE CHURCH is situated at the end of Forth Street, and was opened in 1845. A square tower with a spire recently added is a prominent feature of this building. It also claims to possess special interest in this way.

Soon after the Disruption of 1843, Mr James Crawford, W.S., at that time of the Rhodes, conceived the idea of building a Free Church in North Berwick, in commemoration of the Martyrs of the Bass, because, as he believed, the principles for which the Martyrs suffered were the same as those for which the Free Church had seceded. This was the object set forth on the collecting cards circulated among his friends, which bore the picture of the Bass. And it was to raise funds for this purpose that he persuaded his friends M'Crie the Historian, Anderson the Martyrologist, Hugh Miller the Geologist, and Professors Fleming and Balfour to unite together in writing that most exhaustive and interesting of all books on the Bass "The Bass Rock." Ministers— Senior, Rev. John Shewan ; Junior, Rev. James Davidson, M.A., B.D. Hours of service on Sabbath, 11.15 A.M. and 6 P.M.

In the main street and almost exactly in the centre of the town stands the UNITED PRESBYTERIAN CHURCH of the Martyrs. The present building was opened in 1868 during the tenure of office of the late Rev. W. Calvert, B.A., and it is the third in which the congregation has worshipped. It is a large and handsome structure, and in its conspicuous position it forms one of the attractions of the town. The style is Gothic, and the architect was the late Mr R. R. Raeburn. Two marble memorial tablets are inserted in the wall of the entrance porch. That to the right is inscribed to the memory of the late B. Hall Blyth, Esq., C.E. The slab to the left commemorates the virtues of the Rev. G. Brown, for thirty-six years one of the ministers of North Berwick. He was a member of a highly distinguished Scottish family, which has numbered among its representatives names still well-known in theology and literature, medicine, and science .His father and brother were eminent commentators, and the celebrated author of " Horæ Subsecivæ," and "Rab " was his nephew. The interior of the church is pleasing, the decorations are tasteful, and the seats comfortable. There are several stained glass memorial windows. Hours of service, 11.15 A.M. and 6 P.M. Weekly devotional meeting on Wednesdays at 8. P.M. Minister—Rev. J. D. Robertson, M.A., D.Sc., Edinburgh.

The EPISCOPAL CHURCH OF ST BALDRED, which adjoins the railway station, is a fine Norman edifice, erected in 1861-2, and enlarged in 1863 ; and also in 1885 and 1890. It now holds close on 800 worshippers. The church was originally called All Saints, but at the final consecration it was dedicated to St Baldred, the Hermit of the Bass. The interior of the church is handsomely decorated, the windows being filled with fine stained glass. The south-west window was erected in memory of the officers of the 71st Highlanders, who perished in the Crimea and other parts of the world. The church possesses a sweet-toned organ, presented by Lady Frances Dalrymple. The hours of service are

—Daily, during the summer months, at 8 A.M.; Holy Communion, every Thursday at 8 A.M. Sundays—Holy Communion, 8.30; Matins and Holy Communion, 11 A.M.; Evensong, 6 P.M. Rector—The Rev. F. L. M. Anderson, B.A., Worcester College, Oxford.

The ROMAN CATHOLIC CHURCH, "Our Lady Star of the Sea," is a pretty Gothic building in Law Road, a short distance south of the town. The nave of the church was opened in 1879, and the chancel and sacristry in 1890. This latter portion was designed by Mr Basil Champneys, London, and is well worthy of the architect's reputation. There is a finely carved stone front to the choir gallery. The transept has yet to be added before the proportions of this pretty little church can be properly seen. Hours of service—Sundays, Holy Communion, 9 A.M.; Mass and Sermon, 11 A.M.; Evening Service, 6 P.M. Week-days, Mass, 8 A.M. Priest—Rev. Colin C. M'Kenzie.

DIRLETON PARISH CHURCH (All Saints), two miles from North Berwick (*see* page 43). Service at 12 noon. Parish Minister—The Rev. John Kerr, M.A., Edin.

A new church (St Andrews) was erected at GULLANE in this parish in 1888, being built of stone obtained in the locality. An interesting feature in the structure is the reproduction of the chancel arch from the old Norman ruin in the village, which was once the Parish Church. Service every Sunday at 3 P.M.

POSTAL ARRANGEMENTS.

Box closes for all parts, 8.20 and 11 A.M.; 1.50, 3.20, 6 P.M.; Sundays, 1.50 P.M. Deliveries commence 7 and 9 A.M., 3.45 and 7 P.M.; no delivery on Sundays, but letters can be had at window from 12.30 to 1.30 P.M. TELEGRAMS, 8 A.M. to 9 P.M.; Sundays, 9 to 10 A.M. Stamps, from 8 A.M. to 9 P.M.; Sundays, 12.30 to 1.30 P.M.

Parcels received from 8 A.M. to 6 P.M.—1 lb., 3d.; every additional lb. or fraction thereof, 1½d.—up to 11 lbs.

GOLF.

THE NEW CLUB admits members by a ballot of the committee. The subscription is £2 per annum. Entry money, £10, 10s. Meetings in March and August. THE TANTALLON CLUB admits members by ballot of the club; subscription, 10s. per annum. There are three meetings during the year—March, June, and October—when the various club medals, &c., are played for. THE LADIES' GOLF CLUB—entrance fee, 2s. 6d.; annual subscription, 5s.

BOATING AND FISHING.

The sea fishing at North Berwick is exceedingly good, and comfortable boats, with skilful boatmen, can be had at a moderate charge. There are no trout streams in the immediate neighbourhood of North Berwick, but an excellent day's fishing can be had on the Whitadder by taking the morning train to Grant's House or Chirnside. By returning with the last train in the evening a long day can

THE LADIES' WALK.

be had on the river. The Tyne, at East Linton, is nearer, but permission must be got from the proprietors, which, however, is frequently granted to respectable strangers. The trout and sea-trout fishing in this river is very good.

NORTH BERWICK LAW.

North Berwick Law, a conical hill of igneous felstone, of volcanic formation, 640 feet in height, rises about half a mile south of the town. The easiest ascent is on the west side. The summit, which can be reached in about fifteen to twenty minutes, commands a magnificent panoramic view of the Firth of Forth, the Fife coast, and the Ochil and Lomond Hills; to the west extend the fertile plains of Haddington, with Arthur's Seat and the spires of Edinburgh in the distance; while to the south stretch the Lammermoors. On the top, from time immemorial, have been mounted a pair of whale's jawbones, which have been renewed from time to time; and there is the ruins of a watch-tower, which was occupied as a signal station during the Napoleonic wars. These "Laws" were probably all used as points for lighting beacon fires, and the name is probably derived from the Anglo-Saxon word *hlæw*, a hill. On the south side of the hill is a quarry of white and red porphyry, of which the houses of the town are principally built.

Round the south and west base of the Law runs the Mill Burn, a streamlet so called from having once driven three mills, the ruins of which still stand on its banks.

This brook wends its way through a picturesque and secluded wooded ravine, through which there is a path called the *Ladies' Walk,* delightfully sheltered in boisterous weather from the wind, and shaded in summer from the

CANTY BAY.

sun. In spring the banks of the glen are dotted with primroses and a profusion of other wild flowers.

EXCURSIONS.

CANTY BAY AND TANTALLON CASTLE.

Two and a half miles east of the town is the picturesque little hamlet of *Canty Bay,* the nearest point to the Bass Rock.

NORTH BERWICK LAW, FROM TANTALLON TERRACE.

A short distance beyond the bay, in a commanding position, on a steep rock overhanging the sea, are the fine ruins
of *Tantallon Castle*, so graphically described by Scott in
" Marmion "—   " Tantallon vast ;

> Broad, massive, high, and stretching far,
> And held impregnable in war,
> On a projecting rock it rose,
> And round three sides the ocean flows,
> The fourth did battled walls enclose,
>> And double mound and fosse.
> By narrow drawbridge, outworks strong,
> Through studded gates an entrance long,
>> To the main court they cross.
> It was a wide and stately square :
> Around were lodgings fit and fair,
>> And towers of various form,
> Which on the court projected far,
> And broke its lines quadrangular.
> Here was square keep, there turret high,
> Or pinnacle that sought the sky,
> Whence oft the warder could discry,
>> The gathering ocean-storm."

Canto V. xxxiii.

The date of the building of the castle is lost in obscurity.
It first belonged to the Earls of Fife, and afterwards to the
Menteiths. At the death of Murdoch, Duke of Albany,
it was forfeited to the crown, and given to the Douglas
family, who made it their principal castle. After the banishment of the Earl of Angus in 1527, it was besieged by
James V. ; but, notwithstanding that the King brought
against it two great cannons from the castle of Dunbar—
" thrawn-mouthed Meg and her marrow, and two great
botcards, two moyan, two double falcons, and two quarter

THE HARBOUR.

falcons," the castle remained impregnable. It was, however, shortly afterwards surrendered through the treachery of its governor, Simon Panango. On the return of the Earl of Angus from banishment, and the restitution of his estates, the castle was restored and greatly improved and strengthened. Here, at this time, lived Sir Ralph Sadler, the English Ambassador, during his unsuccessful negotiations for mating the infant, Princess Mary, with Edward VI. The castle was finally dismantled by the Parliamentarians under General Monk, the Douglas who was then in possession being a royalist. At the commencement of last century the castle, along with estate of North Berwick, was purchased by Sir Hew Dalrymple, Lord President of the Court of Session, to whose lineal descendant, the present Sir Walter Hamilton Dalrymple, it still belongs.

On the south side is a deep natural moat, in which was the outer courtyard, one tower of which is still standing. The inner court, in which were the stables and domestic offices, were reached through an archway. On the north the castle was defended by an artificial moat, where can still be seen the piers of the drawbridge. The main entrance to the castle to which the drawbridge led has been built up, and we now enter through a narrow wicket. Over this entrance is the famous "Bloody Heart" of the Douglases, though the emblem is now almost effaced from the armorial shield. From the great tower in the centre extends on either side to the edge of the rock a solid curtain of masonry, fifty feet in height, flanked by lofty towers. The castle buildings extended round three sides of a square. The chapel was in the east wing, and in the west wing traces are still to be seen of the banqueting hall, with the cellars beneath. From its great strength the castle gave rise to the local proverb—"Ding doun Tantallon, and build a brig to the Bass,"—as being both impossibilities. The castle has been lately renovated, and preserved from becoming an utter ruin. A small charge is made for admission.

THE BASS ROCK.

The stupendous isolated crag of the Bass Rock rises from the sea about two miles distant from Canty Bay. The rock, which is about one mile in circumference and 313 feet in height, is a mass of basalt, with precipitous sides rising directly from the sea. The earliest notice of the Bass in history is in connection with the hermit, St Baldred of the Bass, an anchorite who lived here in strict seclusion, according to Hollingshed, in the seventh century, but according to other authorities, in the eighth. In the Breviary of Aberdeen we are told that " there was a great rock between the said island (Bass) and the adjacent land, which remained fixed in the middle of the passage unmoved by all the force of the waves, giving the greatest hindrance to navigation, and often causing shipwrecks. The blessed Baldred, moved by piety, ordered that he should be placed on this rock. This being done, at his word the rock was

immediately lifted up, and, like a ship driven by a favour-
able breeze, proceeded to the nearest shore, and henceforth
remained in the same place as a memorial of this miracle,
and is to this day called St Baldred's coble or cock-boat."
This rock is situated at the mouth of Auldhame Bay, and
is still called " Baudron's Boat." Another legend tells us
that, at the death of the saint, the people of three parishes,
Auldhame, Tyninghame, and Preston, wished to have
the honour of possessing his body. By mutual arrangement they agreed to leave his body unburied for a certain
time, and wait for a sign from Heaven to show which should
be the favoured parish. The very next morning, however,
" three bodies were found instead of one, perfectly alike,
and the people of each parish carried one to their own
church, keeping it there in great honour and veneration for
the miracles that at each place it pleased God to work."
The little chapel on the Bass, portions of the masonry of
which are evidently of Culdee origin, may quite probably
have been the chapel of St Baldred.

In the fourteenth century the Lothians formed part of
the diocese of St Andrews, and a charter is still existing,
dated 4th of June 1316, in which William de Lamberton,
Bishop of St Andrews, grants "to Robert Lauder, for his
homage and service, the whole of our part of the island in
the sea which is called the Bass." This knight was the
founder of the ancient family of the Lauders of the Bass,
who played an important part in Scottish history. At the

BASS ROCK, FROM MARINE HOTEL.

commencement of the fifteenth century, on it being resolved to send the young Prince James, son of Robert III., and afterwards James I., to be educated at the Court of France, he was taken to the Bass for security against the intrigues of the Duke of Albany while the ships forming the expedition were being got ready. Our readers will remember how, after the departure of the expedition, the truce between Scotland and England was violated by the capture of the Prince's ship off Flamborough Head, and how James was kept a prisoner in England for eighteen years, during which time, however, he was kindly treated by his captors, and received an excellent education in the arts and sciences, obtaining also a large experience in politics, which resulted in his eventually becoming one of the wisest and best of the Scottish Kings.

For several centuries after this the Bass continued to be one of the principal strongholds in Scotland, and was often used as a prison for English captives in the wars with England. In October 1571, the rock was sold to the Government, and converted into a state prison at an expense of £4000, in which many of the Covenanters were imprisoned and treated with the greatest cruelty during the dreadful " killing time."

The following extracts from the late Hugh Miller's " Geology of the Bass " give a graphic description of the rock :—" The sloping acclivity of the Bass consists of three great steps or terraces, with steep belts of precipice rising between, and of these terraces the lowest is occupied by the

fortress, and furnishes, where it sinks slopingly to the south-east, the two landing-places of the island. I was not fortunate enough to effect a landing in the great cavern by which the island is perforated, . . . but we approached as near as the straight vestibule, half blocked up by a rock, that at every recession of the wave showed its pointed tusk above the water, gave permission, and I saw enough of the cave to enable me to conceive of its true character and formation. One of those silken-sided lines of division, so common in the trap rocks, runs across the island from west to east, cutting it into two unseparated parts immediately under the foundation of the old chapel. As is not uncommon along these lines, whether occasioned by the escape of vapours from below or the introduction of moisture from above, the rock on both sides, so firm and unwasted elsewhere, is considerably decomposed, and the sea, by incessantly charging direct in the softened line from the stormy east, has, in the lapse of ages, hollowed a passage for itself through a fine natural niche, a full hundred feet in height, which forms the opening of the cavern—the roof bristling high overhead with minute tufts of a beautiful rock-fern, the basement course, if I may so speak, roughened with brown algæ, and having the dark green sea for its floor. But the cavern beyond seems scarce worthy of such a gateway ; the roof appears from this point to close in upon it, and a projection from one of the sides, completely shuts up its long vista to the sea and the daylight on the opposite side of the island. The height of this tunnel of Nature's forming is about 30 feet throughout, its length about 170 yards. It is a dark and dreary recess, full of chill airs and dropping damps—such a cavern as that into which the famous Sinbad the Sailor was lowered at the command of his dear friend the king, when his wife had died, and agreeably to the courtesy of the country, he had to be buried alive in order to keep her company.

" All the doors of the deserted fortalice were open except one, by which the tenant of the Bass fenced against unauthorised visitors the upper part of the island, with its flocks of unfledged gannets and its sheep; and this door, as it occurred not in the transverse wall, but at the top of a long ascending passage beyond, left the space in front of the longitudinal rampart as open to the vagrant foot as the shelving points in front of the transverse one. This door divided the island into two unequal parts, a lower and upper. I am thus particular in detailing the circumstances, as it serves to show on what slight and trivial causes the preservation or extinction of a vegetable species may sometimes depend. The sheep were restricted by the door to the upper division of the island, while two comparatively rare plants, indigenous to the place, the sea beet and the Bass mallow, were found only on its lower division." On the summit of the rock is a heap of stones erected by the Ordnance Survey.

During certain seasons the Bass Rock is the home of myriads of water-fowl; in May and June every available crevice, and even the surface of the island itself, being occupied by nests, eggs, and young birds, while the parents hover and sail around the rock in dense clouds. Notable among the many varieties of sea-birds which breed on the rock is the gannet or solan goose. These birds build their nests of grass or sea-weed on the bare rock or earth, and lay but one egg, from which they are supposed to take the name of *solan*. The young birds when hatched are simply a mass of fat, covered with a very soft white down, and it is from this down that the tenant of the island principally pays his rent. The "harvest" or "harrying" of the birds, as it is called, is a very interesting sight. The men are let down from the top of the precipices by ropes, and, visiting nest after nest, knock the young birds on the head and throw them into the sea below, where they are picked up by their fellow-workers in boats. The full-grown bird measures about six feet from tip to tip of the wings when outstretched, and is white all over, except the pinion feathers of the wings, which are black, and the head and neck, which are of a yellowish tinge. Their food is entirely fish, and in the process of feeding the parent bird brings in its gorge to the nest four or five herrings or sprats, which the young birds pull out with their long pincer-like bills.

A steam launch can be hired at Canty Bay during the season to visit the Bass Rock at all states of the tide, weather permitting. Parties of ten or under, 10/; over that number, 1/ per head. This charge includes sailing round and landing on the rock, and, when circumstances will permit, one of the boatmen will conduct visitors to the different points of interest on the island. Special arrangements can also be made to convey parties direct from North Berwick Harbour to the Rock.

Directly opposite North Berwick is the island of Craigleith, an almost barren rock about a mile in circumference, and only inhabited by rabbits and sea-fowl. The island formerly belonged to the town of Berwick, but the Town Council, being in straits for money, in 1814 tried to dispose of it by means of a lottery, on which being found illegal, they sold it to Sir Hew Dalrymple for £400, and the late Sir John Dalrymple presented it to the Coast Guard of North Berwick.

The largest of the islands near North Berwick is the Isle of Fidra, which lies opposite Dirleton, about a mile from the shore. The western portion is of considerable elevation, and is connected by an isthmus with the eastern part, which rises in castellated form, and is locally called the Castle of Tarbet. In the isthmus is a large cavern into which the sea, in boisterous weather, dashes with great force, producing a noise like thunder. Here seals and myriads of sea-birds make their home. On the north-eastern part of the island a lighthouse and fog-signal station have been erected.

AULDHAME AND SEACLIFF.

About one mile beyond Tantallon is the Castle of

Auldhame, which is a favourite excursion for North Berwick visitors. The castle-yard is covered with fine turf, affording a delightful pic-nicking ground, while seats have been erected by the proprietor, Andrew Laidlay, Esq. Below the castle, near the shore, is the rock referred to on page 34, which commands a beautiful panoramic view of the Bass, Tantallon Castle, the Isle of May, and the Fife coast. A favourite stroll from here is to "St Baldred's Cradle," a creek through which the waves in rough weather rush with great violence. Here St Baldred is said to have been "rocked by the wind and the waves." A short distance to the east of Tantallon Castle is a dilapidated ruin called "Auldhame Church," which is said to have been for some time the abode and the place of the death of St Baldred.

Near Auldhame, a short distance inland, is *Seacliff House*, the seat of A. Laidlay, Esq.

WHITEKIRK.

About five miles distant from North Berwick, and three miles inland from Tantallon, is the old Church of Whitekirk. In 1294, Ann, Countess of Dunbar, after her heroic defence of Dunbar Castle against the troops of Edward I., seeing that further resistance was useless, tried to escape to Fife, but was driven by contrary winds on to the coast near Tantallon. On getting into the boat she was severely hurt, and, being carried ashore in an almost dying state, she prayed to the Virgin for relief. In answer to her supplications, a servant was commissioned by Heaven to tell her that if she would drink of the waters of a well at Fairknowe, near the site of the present church, she would be immediately healed. In faith she followed the advice of the hermit, and no sooner had she drunk of the waters than she was perfectly restored to health. In gratitude for this miracle the Countess built a Chapel and Chantry, and endowed it in honour of the Virgin. The shrine afterwards became of great celebrity, and during the fourteenth and fifteenth centuries was visited annually by many thousands of pilgrims. In 1430 the chapel was taken under the protection of James I., the founder of Holyrood Abbey, who added to it a number of houses for the reception of pilgrims. At the same time he affiliated it with the Abbey of Holyrood, and named it the White Chapel. The prosperity of the little pilgrimage church continued till the reign of Henry VIII., when, on the suppression of the ecclesiastical establishments, the White Chapel was desecrated, the pilgrims' houses were pulled down, and the shrines destroyed, and, on the establishment of the Protestant religion, the chapel was converted into the Parish Church, and called the " White Kirk."

DIRLETON AND GULLANE.

Three miles west of North Berwick is the picturesque village of Dirleton, which is unquestionably one of the prettiest villages in the kingdom. Overshadowed by the noble ruins of Dirleton Castle, with its extensive gardens, and surrounded by quaint and picturesque villas and cottages, the village green forms a most striking and beautiful picture. The Castle of Dirleton was erected in the thirteenth century by the once powerful family of De Vaux. In 1298 it held out for Wallace against Edward I., but, after a stubborn resistance, it was obliged to surrender. It afterwards passed into the possession of the Ruthven family, and was the bribe which induced the laird of Restalrig to join the Gowrie conspiracy. The Castle was finally dismantled and reduced to its present ruinous condition by the Roundhead General Lambert. Visitors are admitted to the castle and its beautiful grounds on Thursdays. The Castle is the property of Mrs Hamilton Ogilvie of Belhaven and Dirleton, to whom visitors are indebted for the privilege of seeing the gardens and grounds, and whose mansion of Archerfield is visible from the Castle walls.

Adjoining Archerfield is a private Golf Course of eighteen holes, under the charge of a local Golf Club. Secretary—T. D. Thomson, Esq., Craigville. This Course is not the least interesting of the many which abound in the neighbourhood. On Thursdays the Parish Church is also open to visitors, and is well worthy of inspection. It dates from 1612, up till which time the church of the parish was at Gullane. The transference to Dirleton was made by an Act of Parliament, because at that time " Gullane was ane decayin place, and Dirleton was ane thrivin toun."

This state of matters has been so far changed that it has been found necessary again to have a church at Gullane.

About a mile and a half beyond Dirleton is the village of Gullane, at which are picturesque ruins of the old Parish Church, which are of great antiquity. It is re-corded that the last vicar of Gullane was deposed by James VI. for smoking tobacco, to which that monarch held a mortal antipathy. Gullane Hill is celebrated for its extensive rabbit warren of 2000 acres. Near Gullane are the ruins of Saltcoats Castle, which was the seat of the ancient family of Livingstone, the founder of whom received a grant of all the lands lying between Gullane Point and North Berwick for having slain a ferocious wild boar which infested the neighbourhood. The glove with which the Livingstone protected his arm in the combat was sold about ninety years ago, and his helmet and spear hung in the family pew in Gullane Church for many years. Skirting the shore, between Gullane and Aberlady Bay, are the celebrated Luffness golfing links, a favourite resort for Edinburgh golfers. At the head of Aberlady Bay, sur-rounded by beautiful grounds, is Luffness House, the residence of H. W. Hope, Esq.

BALGONE AND LUCHIE.

Three miles south of North Berwick is Balgone House, the seat of Sir George Grant Suttie, Bart. The house is surrounded by beautifully laid out and extensive

DIRLETON CASTLE.

grounds, to which, through the courtesy of the proprietor, respectable strangers are admitted on presentation of card at the lodge. In the grounds is a pretty artificial lake nearly half a square mile in extent, which is enlivened by numbers of water-fowl. This is one of the most favourite excursions from North Berwick.

Combined with this excursion a visit can be made to *Luchie House*, the seat of Sir Hew Dalrymple, presently occupied by his widow. The house, which was erected in 1777, is surrounded by beautifully wooded grounds and prettily laid out gardens. Visitors are freely permitted to walk in the park.

TYNINGHAME.

Beautifully situated on the bank of the river Tyne, about six miles south-east of North Berwick, and three miles from East Linton Station, is Tyninghame House, the seat of the Earl of Haddington. The beautiful gardens and magnificent woods surrounding the house are open to visitors on Saturdays. A special feature in the grounds is a fine bowling-green, on which a match is played every year by the bowling clubs of the county to compete for a handsome silver cup presented by the Earl. The house contains some good portraits by Reynolds, Raeburn, &c., and the celebrated picture of " The Gamblers," by Quentin Matsys. The neighbourhood of Tyninghame is celebrated for its holly hedges, which, in some cases, are over twenty-four feet in height and twelve feet in thickness.

LONGNIDDRY AND GOSFORD HOUSE.

The next station to Drem, on the main line to Edinburgh, is Longniddry, a quaint little old-fashioned village. John Knox was tutor in the family of the laird of Longniddry from 1543 to 1547, and is said to have preached his first sermon in the Parish Church. Near the station is the entrance lodge to *Gosford House*, one of the seats of the Earl of Wemyss. A new residence has just been finished near the site of the old house. The house contains a fine gallery of pictures by old masters.

HADDINGTON.

Haddington can be reached by rail from North Berwick *via* Drem and Longniddry, or by a carriage drive of ten miles. The town is prettily situated on the banks of the Tyne, and is celebrated as being the birthplace of John Knox, who first saw the light of day in a cottage (now pulled down) near the Parish Church. The house was in a field, which is pointed out to visitors—a tree marking the spot where the house stood. Haddington was also the birthplace of Dr Samuel Smiles, the author of " Self-Help." The Parish Church was formerly the nave of a stately Franciscan Abbey, the choir and transepts of which are now ruinous, but shortly to be restored. In the churchyard is the tomb of Jane Welsh, wife of Thomas Carlyle.

DUNBAR.

There is no more pleasant excursion from North Berwick than the drive to Dunbar through Binning Woods, a distance of eleven miles. The town can also be reached in a short time by rail *via* Drem. Carlyle, in his "Cromwell," thus describes it—"The small town of Dunbar stands, high and windy, looking down over its herring boats, over its grim old castle now much honeycombed, on one of those projecting rock promontories with which that shore of the Firth of Forth is niched and vandyked as far as the eye can reach. A beautiful sea . . . a grim niched barrier of whinstone sheltering it from the chafings and tumblings of the big blue German Ocean." The town principally consists of one long street, at the extremity of which is Dunbar House, formerly a noble residence, built by James Fall, a Dunbar merchant and member for the boroughs, but now a barrack. On the bankruptcy of the son of Mr Fall, in 1788, the house was purchased by the eighth Earl of Lauderdale, and was for some time a residence of the Lauderdale family. Behind this building are the ruins of Dunbar Castle, once one of the most famous strongholds in Scotland, but now only a few fragments of masonry on a red sandstone rock hollowed by the waves into an arch. The castle was the scene of several of the most important events in the English wars in the time of Bruce. It was captured by Edward I. in 1296, and Edward II. fled hither after the battle of Bannockburn in 1314; but the most celebrated event connected with the castle was its heroic defence by "Black Agnes," Countess of March, in 1339. The Earl of Salisbury, after trying in vain to capture the castle, was compelled to raise the siege, after which the town was made a royal borough by David II. In 1566 the governorship of the castle was conferred on the Earl of Bothwell by Queen Mary, "who was carried off from Edinburgh by him and an armed band under his orders to his castle, April 22, 1567, after the murder of Darnley, and only three weeks before her marriage with Bothwell. Accompanied by Darnley, she had taken refuge here after the murder of Rizzio; and hither again she fled, in the disguise of a page, with Bothwell, after the interruption of their honeymoon at Borthwick Castle. A few days afterwards she surrendered at Carberry Hill, and Dunbar Castle was destroyed by the Regent Moray." A favourite place of resort is the castle park, which commands a fine view ever the sea and harbour.

FORTH BRIDGE.

This, the most wonderful and gigantic of all engineering achievements, can easily be visited from North Berwick in one day by taking train to Edinburgh, and thence taking advantage of one of the many means of reaching it from that city.

MARINE HOTEL.

PRESS NOTICES.

" We prefer the splendid Marine, which is altogether one of the best hostelries we have ever visited. It is close to the links and contains all that the heart of man could desire, from French cookery to electric bells."—*Whitehall Review*, 19th August, 1880.

"The commodious and admirably-managed Marine Hotel." —*Daily News*, 23rd August, 1886.

"Its rooms are lofty and well ventilated, the attendance good, the *cuisine* superior, and the charges moderate."—*Belfast News Letter*, 14th April, 1887.

"Residence at the Marine Hotel, from the gardens of which you step forth on the golfing links, is one of the most pleasant of my holiday recollections. . . . The sanitary arrangements of the building are perfect."—Dr Andrew Wilson in *Health*, 19th August, 1887.

"Last of all, but by no means least, there is a very large, ably-managed and excellent Hotel at North Berwick, the Marine Hotel, where every look through the windows on a fine day really seems a framed water-colour, so bright are the glimpses of greensward, the blue sea, and Italian-like sky."—*The World*, 14th September, 1887.

CAB FARES

From the Marine Hotel to Places of Interest and Back.

	Miles.	£	s.	d.
ARCHERFIELD HOUSE	3½	0	5	0
ABERLADY and BAY	8	0	12	0
AULDHAME (Wednesday)	4	0	6	0
BALGONE HOUSE	3	0	4	6
CANTY BAY, for BASS ROCK	3	0	4	6
DIRLETON GARDENS (Thursday)	3	0	4	6
DREM	6	0	9	0
DUNBAR	12	0	17	0
GULLANE	5	0	7	6
GOSFORD HOUSE (Earl of Wemyss)	9	0	14	0
HADDINGTON	10	0	15	0
LUCHIE HOUSE (Lady Dalrymple)	2½	0	3	6
LUFFNESS (H. W. Hope, Esq.)	7	0	10	0
NEWBYTH (Sir David Baird)	6	0	9	0
PRESSMENNAN and LAKE	14	1	0	0
SEACLIFFE (A. Laidlay, Esq.)	4½	0	7	0
TANTALLON CASTLE	3	0	4	6
TYNINGHAME and BINNING WOODS	7	0	10	0
WHITEKIRK	5	0	7	6
WHITTINGHAME	10	0	15	0

If the journey is under 10 miles, half-an-hour's wait free of charge.
If over 10 miles, two hours free; after that, 2s. an hour.
Shopping and making calls in Town—Forenoon, 2s. 6d. an hour;
Afternoon, 3s. 6d. an hour.
Single Fares, 1s. per mile; Return, 1s. 6d., for One Horse. Pair of
Horses, half-fare extra.

Drive round by TANTALLON and LUCHIE LODGE ...	£0	6	0
„ TANTALLON, WHITEKIRK, BALGONE, and LUCHIE	0	7	6
„ DIRLETON, FENTONBARNS, KINGSTON, and LAW	0	7	0
„ DIRLETON, GULLANE, LUFFNESS, and DREM	0	11	0

Tourists' Tickets, available for *Two Calendar Months, are issued from Glasgow, &c.

TO NORTH BERWICK—AS UNDER—

FROM	1 Cl. s. d.	2 Cl. s. d.	3 Cl. s. d.
Glasgow (Queen Street, Bellgrove, College, Charing Cross, Finnieston, Yorkhill, Partick, Hyndland, Great Western Rd., Maryhill and Cowlairs)	12 6	..	6 6
Craigendoran Pier & Helensburgh	14 3	..	7 6
Dumbarton	14 3	..	7 6
Balloch	14 3	..	7 6
Alexandria	14 3	..	7 6
Falkirk	12 0	..	6 0
Grahamston	12 0	..	6 0
Polmont	10 6	..	5 6
Linlithgow	9 6	..	5 0
Bathgate (Upper)	9 6	..	5 0
Stirling	12 6	..	6 6
Alloa via Larbert	12 6	..	6 6
Alva via Larbert	12 6	..	6 6
Menstrie via Larbert	12 6	..	6 6
Dollar	13 0	..	7 0
Tillicoultry	13 0	..	7 0
Dundee (Tay-Br. Stn.) via Granton	16 6	..	8 0
Perth via Granton	16 6	..	8 0
Aberdeen via Granton	36 0	..	18 0
Arbroath via Granton	19 9	..	9 7
Broughty via Granton	16 6	..	8 0
Montrose	24 6	..	12 0
St Andrews, via Granton	16 6	..	8 0

FROM	1 Cl. s. d.	2 Cl. s. d.	3 Cl. s. d.
Cupar via Granton	15 3	..	7 0
Dunfermline and Comely Park	10 9	..	6 0
Leven via Granton	11 3	..	6 0
Methil via Granton	11 3	..	6 0
Thornton Granton	10 9	..	6 0
Kirkcaldy	9 0	..	4 3
Hawick	16 6	11 9	9 0
Berwick	10 0	8 0	6 0
Canobie	25 6	19 10	11 6
Airdrie (South)	12 6	..	6 6
Coatbridge (Sunnyside)	12 6	..	6 6
Whiffet	12 6	..	6 6
Bellshill	12 6	..	6 6
Maryville	12 6	..	6 6
Uddingstone	12 6	..	6 6
Hamilton	12 6	..	6 6
Peacock Cross	12 6	..	6 6
Bothwell	12 6	..	6 6
*Carlisle	28 6	21 3	14 3
*Hexham	32 8	25 6	18 6
*Alnwick	19 6	16 0	10 11
*Darlington	38 2	31 6	20 9
*Durham	32 6	26 8	18 0
*Morpeth	23 6	19 2	13 0
*Newcastle	27 8	22 8	15 6
*Northallerton	42 0	34 8	23 0
*Thirsk	44 0	36 4	24 0
*York	50 0	41 4	27 0

*Tourists Tickets from Stations in England to North Berwick are valid until 31st December.

Passengers holding the above tickets are entitled to break the journey at any passing station in going or returning.

On previous application to the General Superintendent, North British Railway, Edinburgh, arrangements will be made for the stoppage at Drem of any of the Down East Coast Express Trains (excepting the 10 A.M. from King's Cross) to set down passengers for North Berwick.

For Train arrangements between Stations in England and North Berwick see the Time Tables of the Great Northern, North Eastern, and Midland Railway Companies.

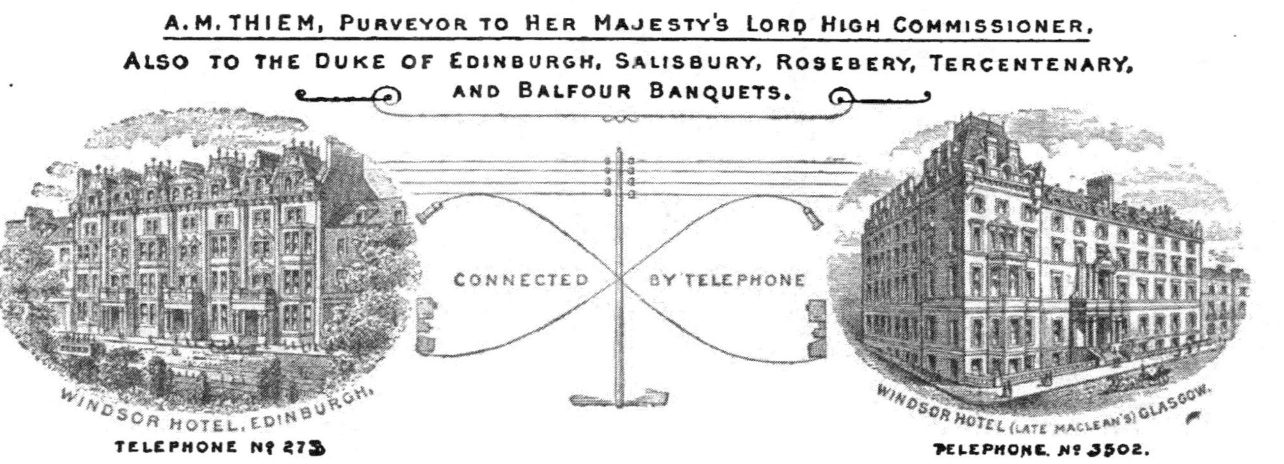

THE WINDSOR HOTELS, EDINBURGH AND GLASGOW

FIRST-CLASS HOTELS FOR FAMILIES AND GENTLEMEN

A. M. THIEM. Proprietor

EDWIN BENNETT
WATCH AND CLOCK MAKER
NORTH BERWICK

Jewellery Repaired.   Clocks wound and kept by the year.

Clocks and Watches Cleaned and Repaired on the Premises

**Glass, China, Earthenware, and Fancy Goods
kept in Stock**

DALRYMPLE ARMS HOTEL
AND POSTING ESTABLISHMENT
NORTH BERWICK

LANDAUS

WAGGONETTES

CHAPEL CARTS

Large Brake for Picnic Parties

STABLING, &c.

J. M'AINSH, Proprietor

JOHN R. WHITECROSS

Dealer in First-Class

FAMILY GROCERIES & PROVISIONS

Wine Merchant and Italian Warehouseman

HIGH STREET AND WEST END

NORTH BERWICK

Importer of

Sherries, Ports, Clarets, Brandies, and Liqueurs

Agent for   **BURGOYNE'S**
GOLD MEDAL

AUSTRALIAN WINES

MAX GREGER'S

HUNGARIAN WINES

RAGGETT'S

CELEBRATED

NOURISHING LONDON STOUT

A Special Blend of very Old Matured

SCOTCH MALT WHISKY

18/- per Gallon.   36/- per Dozen.

THREE DOZEN AND UPWARDS CARRIAGE PAID.

ALEXANDER MERRILEES

Boot and Shoe Maker

HIGH STREET

NORTH BERWICK

Repairs Neatly Executed at Moderate Prices

Boots and Shoes of every Description Ready-Made or to Order

Warrender House Private Hotel

NORTH BERWICK.

The situation is first-class, and commands beautiful views of the Firth of Forth, Fife Coast, and Lomond Hills.

CHARGES STRICTLY MODERATE

Within Three Minutes' Walk from Railway Station, and contiguou to Golf Links.

For Particulars apply to the Proprietress.

WAMPHRAY

 DAIRY

DALRYMPLE BUILDINGS

NORTH BERWICK

****

Milk and Cream

DELIVERED TO ALL PARTS OF THE TOWN

Fresh Butter and Eggs

****

JOHN CLARK

WAMPHRAY

BRODIE

HOUSE AGENT

NORTH BERWICK

BRODIE

Baker & Confectioner

NORTH BERWICK

Manufacturer of Celebrated Tantallon Cakes

(SUPPLIED TO HER MAJESTY)

BRODIE

POSTMASTER

NORTH BERWICK

GEORGE SIM

DRAPER AND CLOTHIER
17 HIGH STREET
NORTH BERWICK

INVITES attention to his Large and Fashionable Stock of DRAPERY GOODS—at all times replete with the Latest Novelties in Style and Fashion—carefully selected at the Principal Markets, and, being bought on the best terms, Purchasers will find the value unequalled by any in the Trade.

In connection with the Establishment, G. S. employs a staff of

Milliners, Dressmakers, and Tailors

each Department being superintended by thoroughly competent Managers. Orders punctually executed in the Latest Styles. *Superior Finish and Correct Fit guaranteed.*

CHARGES STRICTLY MODERATE

THE FANCY DEPARTMENT

Contains Large Selections in FANCY APRONS and PINAFORES, LADIES' UNDERCLOTHING, CHILDREN'S DRESSES, GLOVES of every Description, UMBRELLAS, AND SUNSHADES.

Fancy Collar and Cuff Sets, Frillings, Ribbons, Laces, Smallwares, &c.

HOUSEHOLD DRAPERY

Contains a large Stock of CALICOES, FLANNELS, SHEETINGS, BATH TOWELS, TABLE CLOTHS, &c., exceptionally good value.

SPECIALITY

A Large Stock of BATHING GOWNS, COMBINATIONS, and COSTUMES, made on the Premises, at various Prices; also, a Large Selection of WATERPROOF BATHING CAPS.

INSPECTION RESPECTFULLY INVITED

GEORGE SIM, 17 High St., North Berwick

THOMAS HIMSWORTH

Joiner and Cabinetmaker

WEST END

NORTH BERWICK

<hr>

Agent for Paterson & Sons' Pianofortes

<hr>

WINDOWS GLAZED & CLEANED

FIREWOOD

<hr>

Houses looked after during Winter Months

JAMES BURNETT

Cab Proprietor

79 WESTGATE

(Opposite New Parish Church)

NORTH BERWICK

FOR HIRE—

LANDAU CARRIAGES, WAGGONETTES, LARGE
BRAKE FOR PICNIC PARTIES, DOG-CARTS, ETC.

Light Lorry for Removing Luggage and Furniture

HORSBURGH

(FROM J. ALLAN & SON, EDINBURGH)

BOOTMAKER

12 WEST GATE, NORTH BERWICK

Local Agent for "Scafe's Patent" Combination, Golfing,
Shooting, and Walking Boots

Repairs of every Description efficiently and promptly executed

WHITE STAR LINE

ROYAL AND UNITED STATES MAIL STEAMERS.

Sailing every WEDNESDAY between

LIVERPOOL AND NEW YORK

(Calling at QUEENSTOWN for Mails and Passengers).

SALOON FARES

"Majestic" and "Teutonic"

SUMMER SEASON—

£18 to £35 per berth : Deck Rooms and Suites, £80 and upwards.

Return Rates 10 per cent. off Double Fares.

SALOON FARES

By other **Steamers**

£12, £15, £18, and £22 per berth, according to position of berth and number in State-Room, all having equal privileges in the Saloon.

Children under 12 years, Half Fare. Infants under 2 years, Free.

Return Tickets, £24 to £40.

The Magnificent New Twin Screw Steamers, "MAJESTIC" and "TEUTONIC" built by the eminent shipbuilders, Messrs Harland & Wolff, Belfast, each 10,000 tons, are the longest vessels in the world, and will sail regularly in the itinerary of the Line. They are fitted with all the most recent improvements, are luxuriously furnished, and unsurpassed in the excellence of their appointments for the comfort and convenience of passengers.

Second Cabin and Steerage Rates as low as by any other First-Class Line.

For Passage apply to JAMES SCOTT & CO., Queenstown ; GENESTAL & DELZONS, 1 Rue Scribe, Paris ; or to ISMAY, IMRIE & CO., 10 Water Street, Liverpool, And 34 LEADENHALL STREET, LONDON, E.C.

GUION LINE

ROYAL AND UNITED STATES MAIL STEAMERS

N.B.—The "ARIZONA" and "ALASKA" are two of the Faste
Steamers afloat.

From Liverpool to New York every Saturday, calling at Queenstown to embark Passengers.
From New York every Tuesday for Queenstown and Liverpool.

The Steamers of this Line are of the fastest and finest class on the Atlantic ; they ar built in water-tight compartments, and are furnished with every requisite to make the passa across the Atlantic both safe and agreeable. The State-rooms are all on the upper deck, th ensuring those greatest of all luxuries at sea—perfect ventilation and light.

SALOON PASSAGE from Liverpool or Queenstown, £10 to £26 ea berth, according to size, situation, and accommodation of the State-room occupied ; all havi the same privileges in the Saloon. **Children under Twelve, Half-Fare; Infan Free. Return Tickets at Reduced Rates.**

SECOND CABIN (2, 4, and 6 in a room) and Steerage to New Yor Boston, and Philadelphia, at rates as low as by other first-class lines.

Through Bookings to all parts of the United States and Canada.

Passengers for New Zealand, Australia, China, Japan, South Africa, & booked by direct Royal Mail Steamers from London.

For further particulars apply in London, to GUION & Co., 5 Waterloo Place, Pall Ma in Paris, to A. H. GROVES, 5 Rue Scribe ; in Queenstown, to JAMES SCOTT & Co. ; and Liverpool, to

GUION & CO., Drury Buildings, 21 Water Stree

MACKAY, CUNNINGHAM & CO.

JEWELLERS, SILVERSMITHS

WATCH AND CLOCKMAKERS

74 PRINCES STREET

EDINBURGH

One of the Oldest Established Houses in Scotland

AN EXTENSIVE STOCK OF VALUABLE ARTICLES OF

JEWELLERY AND SILVER PLATE

AT REDUCED PRICES

SCOTTISH JEWELLERY
AND PEBBLE ORNAMENTS

In great variety and of the latest designs from
a few Shillings upwards

A Visit of Inspection invited

R. & T. GIBSON

Provision Merchants, Tea and Coffee Salesmen

Grocers and Italian Warehousemen

93 PRINCES STREET

AND

5 FREDERICK STREET
EDINBURGH

~~~~~~~~~~~~~~~~~~~~~~

TERMS—READY MONEY
PRICE LIST ON APPLICATION

~~~~~~~~~~~~~~~~~~~~~~

For the Convenience of Customers

WAITING ROOMS FOR LADIES & GENTLEMEN

have been provided, where Tea and Coffee can be had

John Macintyre

CHEMIST

(From Messrs DUNCAN, FLOCKHART & CO., Edinburgh)

33 HIGH STREET, NORTH BERWICK

RESPECTFULLY assures his friends and the public generally that the greatest care and accuracy are exercised in the Dispensing of Physicians' Prescriptions, and the most approved methods of combination and manipulation adopted.

A thorough knowledge gained in the extensive business of Messrs Duncan, Flockhart & Co., Chemists to the Queen, Edinburgh, secures to his Patrons every possible advantage; and the steady increase of business in the Dispensing Department warrants the belief that strict attention in this direction is fully recognised.

The best Drugs and Chemicals only are employed, the directions and tests of the Pharmacopœia (the legal standard) strictly adhered to, and the purity and uniformity of strength of all Pharmaceutical Preparations are thus guaranteed.

In continuing this course, Mr MACINTYRE hopes to merit an increased patronage, which shall ever have his best personal attention.

BUSINESS HOURS—8.30 a.m. to 8 p.m. Sundays, 10 to 11 a.m. 12.30 to 1.30 p.m.; 7 to 8 p.m.

Iu cases of emergency occurring after business hours, Medicines may be had, and Prescriptions attended to, by applying at the

HOUSE NEXT DOOR

Huddleston & Co

Edinburgh